SHINE

First printed in Australia in 2012

Version 1

ISBN: 978-1-922076-04-5

While the manual is consistent with the values of Hillsong CityCare under the umbrella of Hillsong Church, the program and manual are suitable for use within any value or faith-based system. The purpose of this community development program is to promote holistic, humanitarian and strengths based approach to life.

The program manuals are designed to assist facilitators in achieving the objectives of each session by providing various selections of recommended exercises. These exercises can be replaced with similar type exercises where facilitators assess its appropriateness according to the characteristics of their target group. The program is designed to promote flexibility to facilitators in delivering a custom tailored program whilst ensuring that the exercises used remain consistent with the underlying values and concepts that emerge in this program.

Inquiries should be addressed to:

Hillsong Music Australia, Po Box 1195, Castle Hill NSW 1765, Australia
T: +61 2 8853 5300   F: +61 2 8846 4625   E: resources@hillsong.com

SHINE

MY **SHINEWOMEN** JOURNAL

name & date

C

overview.

ShineWOMEN is a unique personal development and group mentoring tool that uses an inspirational, practical and experiential approach to learning. This program is founded upon the premise that every life counts and has intrinsic value, and fosters an awareness of this belief. As a result, women are equipped to become effective global citizens for the future.

aim.

For each woman to develop understanding of her own personal worth, strength and purpose and realise the potential within her to fulfil her desires.

objectives.

Equip women to:
Identify themselves as valuable with much to contribute
Build confidence, self-esteem and self-worth
Develop respect and boundaries in relationships
Understand they are able to have a positive influence in their world
Identify personal desires and strengths to motivate them to set and achieve personal goals

These message objectives are achieved through:

three foundational concepts. worth. strength. purpose.

i have
WORTH!
'BODY AND SOUL, I AM WONDERFULLY MADE'

The focus for these sessions is for you to understand for yourself that you are valuable.
Your uniqueness is something to celebrate and you have been wonderfully made.

i have
STRENGTH!
'CHOOSE LIFE'

These sessions explore the power of choice and the power that decisions have on shaping a person's future.
This is addressed through practical sessions about feelings, convictions, decision-making and problem-solving.

i have
PURPOSE!
'I HAVE A HOPE AND A FUTURE'

Purpose is examined through exploring personal hopes, dreams and desires. Goal setting, group discussions
on potential talents and practical activities, are used to equip and build
confidence to live out a purpose-filled, adventurous life.

'BODY AND SOUL, I AM WONDERFULLY MADE'

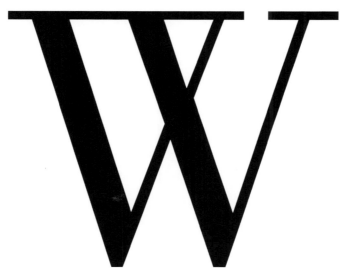

worth.

SESSION ONE I AM VALUABLE
SESSION TWO I AM ONE-OF-A-KIND
SESSION THREE I AM WONDERFULLY MADE

'BODY AND SOUL, I AM WONDERFULLY MADE'

1

worth.

SESSION ONE I AM VALUABLE

outcomes.

By the end of this session, you will be able to:

GAIN AN UNDERSTANDING OF THE CONCEPT OF VALUE

IDENTIFY WHAT YOU PERSONALLY VALUE AND WHY

DEVELOP AN AWARENESS OF PERSONAL VALUE

foundational concept.

Our value has nothing to do with what we think or what people say about us. Our value is not attached to our performance. It is not based on our circumstances, family background, religion or socio-economic status. Human value is not determined by what people say about us. It's not determined by whether we have failed more times than we have succeeded. Our value is not determined by whether we have finished school, have a job, a car, a boyfriend or are well liked. Circumstances like whether we are sick or healthy, rich or poor do not determine our value. Our value is linked to our very being – it is intrinsic. Value cannot be earned, regardless of what circumstances we find ourselves in, we all qualify for value and worth.

Explore the questions: 'Am I accepted? Do I matter? Do you see me? Do you hear me? Does what I am saying matter to you? Do you recognise me? Do your eyes light up when I am around?' Every one of us has this need for acceptance. It's a universal need.

You matter! What you have to say matters.
You are worth being cared about, listened to and validated. You are recognised. You are important.

reflection.

Q. How do hands relate to value?

_____

_____

_____

_____

_____

_____

Q. What do we use our hands for?

_____

_____

_____

_____

_____

_____

Q. What are some things hands can do for people – helping and giving?

_____

_____

_____

_____

_____

_____

Hands were never designed to cause harm to ourselves or to others. Hands are an extension of our gifts and talents into the world. Our hands are designed to serve us well and serve others well in love. A hurting humanity can end up having hands that hurt others, but it's not what our hands are meant to be doing.

Hands are only one part of our amazing body. They are never insignificant and add to our worth as a human being. Every hand not only looks unique and is one-of-a-kind but every hand does unique things.

'BODY AND SOUL, I AM WONDERFULLY MADE'

worth.

SESSION TWO I AM ONE-OF-A-KIND

outcomes.

By the end of this session, you will be able to:

RECOGNISE THE VALUE OF BEING ONE-OF-A-KIND

DISTINGUISH THE DIFFERENCE BETWEEN UNIQUENESS AND COMPARISON

one-of-a-kind is

BEAU
TIFUL

Each of us was born with a one-of-a-kind personality. The way we love is one-of-a-kind. Our personal style and creativity is one-of-a-kind. How we communicate is different. How we write or give expression to something is unique. If a group of people were to write about the same topic, not one paper would be written the same. That is because our personal expression of life is unique and one-of-a-kind.

When something is one-of-a-kind, it is precious and valuable; it is a treasure… it has worth.
Each of us is set apart as unique and there is no one like us! We are born one-of-a-kind, custom-built and a masterpiece!

UNIQUE: a one-off, original, exceptional, rare, unequalled, extraordinary, incomparable, matchless, individual.

We are all different! This is something to celebrate.

DIFFERENT: not the same, unlike, of other nature, form or quality

reflection.

Q. How does my appearance give expression to my one-of-a-kind life?

_____

_____

_____

_____

Q. How does my heritage and culture give expression to my one-of-a-kind life?

_____

_____

_____

_____

Q. How does my personality and character give expression to my one-of-a-kind life?

_____

_____

_____

_____

_____

Q. How does my personal written signature give expression to my one-of-a-kind life?

_____

_____

_____

_____

_____

'BODY AND SOUL, I AM WONDERFULLY MADE'

3

worth.

SESSION THREE I AM WONDERFULLY MADE

outcomes.

By the end of this session, you will be able to:

EXPLAIN YOUR UNDERSTANDING OF THE WORTH CONCEPT

IDENTIFY WAYS TO VALUE YOURSELF

foundational concept.

There are many facets to who we are. Every part of us has a purpose and a function. Our mind, body, emotions, personality, character, passions and dreams are all intricate parts of us.

There are many characteristics that contribute to our individuality: our strengths, talents, laughter and smile have all been uniquely designed just for us. No one else is exactly the same. We have been designed just the way we are for a reason and a purpose.

When we love something, we value it. Anything we love and adore, we treat with value. When we love ourselves, we are valuing ourselves.

The idea of living a life that shines is to see all we do, be about placing value on ourselves and others. We exercise to be strong in the core of our body so that we can be fit to carry on our amazing journey well. We require fuel for the body by eating the right food to keep healthy, as well as limiting chemicals where possible that are harmful for our inner and outer environment.

we are all

PRICE
LESS

ILLUSTRATION: OUR UNIQUENESS

'The arrangement of a human being is so incredible for a reason. As we all know, human beings are made up of many cells but it's what's inside the nucleus that defines who we are and gives us our unique life. In the basic building blocks of matter – The DNA - in a human being, there are four different types of building blocks that pair up with each other so precisely and so specifically such that three of these pairs form one part of a sequence to make our proteins or part of a gene in a specific order. The combination and order of these pairs of blocks is what makes up who you are – your genetic code. This DNA coding is not just for eye colour and hair which relates to your blueprint but DNA is more complex. It has to be...we are very complex. If this is where our code is for the way we are uniquely made, then it also has to be also about how you feel, why you're passionate about certain things. Scientists can't copy it or make it in the lab... it has to come from a creator who designed us to be who we are.'

Dr Bernadette Morris –Smith (2011), PhD Microbiology & Genetics, University of London

ILLUSTRATION: OUR VALUE IS PRICELESS

Human value is not determined by what people say about us. It's not determined by whether or not we have failed more times than we have succeeded. Our value is not determined by whether or not we have finished school, have a job, a car, a boyfriend or are well-liked. Circumstances like whether we are sick or healthy, rich or poor do not determine our value.

If our value is not determined by all these things, then what is it determined by? What price do we put on ourselves?

'CHOOSE LIFE'

strength.

'CHOOSE LIFE'

strength.

SESSION FOUR I HAVE THE POWER OF CHOICE

outcomes.

By the end of this session, you will be able to:

EXPLORE AND UNDERSTAND THAT EVERY WOMAN IS BORN WITH FEELINGS

DEMONSTRATE SKILLS REQUIRED TO ENHANCE THE POWER OF CHOICE

foundational concept.

We have free will – the power to make choices in our lives. Our strength grows when we exercise our will for good, for ourselves and for others. It comes from our daily decision to choose to do what is right for us. What is right looks different for different people. We need to discover what is right for ourselves.

Choices affect our lives and the lives of people around us. No matter how we feel, we have the power to choose our direction in life. This does not mean choices will always be easy. Some of our choices will challenge the very core of who we believe we are. Yet others will be easy. Making right choices in life, especially in difficult situations, builds our strength and our maturity as women. Our decisions can be influenced by others, especially those we love. We can choose to hand our 'power of choice' over to them or we can hold onto it.

We can choose to make each of our experiences in life count. We can't always change our circumstances, but we can take control over what we do about them. We have the CHOICE to: RESPOND to a situation or REACT to it.

Above everything, we hold the power to choose.

managing our emotions.

EMOTION: any strong feeling, such as joy or fear, the part of a person's character based on feelings rather than thought. It's important to recognise how we are feeling.

Feelings should not be ignored or buried. Instead, as we honestly accept our feelings we begin to mature as women. When we identify and acknowledge these feelings it starts the process of disempowering the desire to react so that we can respond to what is happening around us.

It's important to recognise how we are feeling. They are keys to revealing what we think about things - our mindsets and our belief systems. What we think and subsequently feel influences the decisions we make and how we live out our life.

thoughts & beliefs. feelings. decisions. response.
All these things influence our behaviours and actions.

Our thoughts and beliefs influence our feelings, which influence our decision-making. These in turn influence our responses to situations. It's important to maintain a balance when it comes to our emotions and not live a life controlled by them. Our emotions can become like a rollercoaster. If we allow our feelings to get out of balance they can begin to run our lives. In order to keep ourselves balanced we use our emotions to tell us how we are feeling, instead of allowing them to influence our choices in life.

Once we identify our feelings, it may be helpful to explore them further:
Why am I feeling like this? What has caused these feelings? What choices do I have?
Do I need to forgive someone? How can I resolve this? How long have I felt this way? Can I change how I am feeling?

For example: If you're feeling angry, ask yourself:
Why am I angry? Where is this coming from? What has caused this anger? How long has this made me angry?

When we begin to explore our feelings and the reasons behind them, we start to understand our past and our present and look forward to a different future.

STREN GTH IS...

BUILDING ON GOOD RELATIONSHIPS

CHOOSING TO MAKE OUR EXPERIENCES COUNT

LOOKING FOR THE GOOD IN ALL THINGS

ASKING FOR HELP WHEN WE NEED IT

HAVING AN ATTITUDE OF GRATITUDE

RESPONDING AND NOT REACTING TO OUR SITUATION

LIVING A LIFE TRUE TO OUR VALUES AND CONVICTIONS

ALLOWING OTHERS TO COME ALONGSIDE TO SUPPORT US

BELIEVING THE TRUTH ABOUT OURSELVES

HAVING HEALTHY BOUNDARIES AND RESPECT

'CHOOSE LIFE'

5

strength.

SESSION FIVE MY DECISIONS DETERMINE MY DESTINATION

outcomes.

By the end of this session, you will be able to:

APPLY AND PRACTISE DECISION-MAKING SKILLS

RECOGNISE THE VALUE OF RESPECT AND BOUNDARIES

foundational concept.

In every situation, in every day, we make choices. In those choices there are consequences that add to our life moving us forward, and there are consequences that stop us moving at all or cause us to move backwards.

There are decisions that can fast track us on our journey and others that can keep us from it.

Decisions we make give us control over our life; but they don't just affect our life, they also impact the people around us. There are choices that are selfish and those that are selfless.

All the decisions we make – from getting out of bed each morning to who we marry –have consequences. Our choices determine what our tomorrow will look like. Things we decide to overcome and things we decide to accept all have a direct effect on our life. Often we don't realise that it's the small, everyday decisions that get us to our desired destination.

boundaries.

We may hear certain people talk about 'personal boundaries' from time to time. Indeed, boundaries are essential to cultivating a healthy sense of personal worth. But what are they? Why do we need them? How do we set up healthy boundaries?

Boundaries are like maps that show us where we start and finish. Some examples of boundaries in the world include property lines and state borders. Personal boundaries are similar to this. As unique individuals, we each need boundaries for our body, soul and heart to stay healthy.

Boundaries help us take care of our property – we hold onto the things that help us inside our fences and keep things that will hurt us outside. In short, boundaries help us keep the good in and the bad out. Boundaries also help us build a community, and within that community, everyone has their own space and property.

The important idea to remember is that our gates must be flexible enough to allow or prevent entry of influences as we determine.

Some of us have lived a life where we have followed the demands or opinions of others in order to be 'nice people'. As a result, we may have lost ourselves in our efforts to please others and win their approval. Living this way allows frustration, abuse, depression or resentment to take root in our thoughts and emotions.

'Do you believe you have something valuable to offer the world?'

power of choice.

Even with life events that occur in a way that we seemingly don't have a choice over (being laid off work, the car breaking down, a flood, etc.) we still have a choice over how we respond to those events because we know what our boundaries are. We can choose to see things that feel like, and seem to be, tragic as opportunities for growth. Learning to set boundaries is a vital part of learning to communicate in a direct and honest manner. If you have a boundary that involves another person, you need to both agree on this boundary, value it and be accountable.

respect.

*RESPECT: esteem for or a sense of the worth or excellence of a person,
the condition of being esteemed or honoured, to show regard or consideration for.*

*HONOUR: the state of being honoured; the quality of being honourable and having a good name.
Giving worth and weight to what is truly valuable.*

On a practical level, respect includes taking someone's feelings, needs, thoughts, ideas, wishes and preferences into consideration. It means taking all of these seriously and giving them worth and value. In fact, giving someone respect seems similar to valuing them and their thoughts, feelings and so forth. It also includes acknowledging them, listening to them, being truthful with them, and accepting their individuality.

Respect can be shown through behaviour and it can also be felt. We can act in ways which are considered respectful, yet we can also feel respect for someone and feel respected by someone. Because it is possible to act in ways that do not reflect how we really feel, the feeling of respect is more important than the behaviour without the feeling. When the feeling is there, the behaviour will naturally follow.

reflection.

Q. What qualities come naturally to you?

_____

_____

_____

_____

_____

_____

_____

_____

_____

_____

_____

_____

_____

Q. What kind of qualities would you like to develop?

_____

_____

_____

_____

_____

_____

_____

_____

_____

_____

_____

_____

_____

_____

'CHOOSE LIFE'

strength.

SESSION SIX I HAVE RESILIENCE

outcomes.

By the end of this session, you will be able to:

RECOGNISE THE VALUE OF DEVELOPING RESILIENCE

foundational concept...resilience.

RESILIENCE: ability to recover readily from adversity.

Resilience is the strength to withstand adversity. It is the ability to handle difficult situations, people, environments and setbacks.

Being able to bounce back and recover from adversity makes us stronger and contributes to our dreams becoming a reality. A resilient person is able to stand firm whilst facing significant difficulties and stress as they have a strong sense of self-belief and faith in their capabilities.

We need to understand that life will not always be smooth sailing. Life is not always great. Things happen that we would prefer didn't. But if life was always wonderful, would we appreciate all the great things or would we take them for granted? We can learn so much about ourselves when we go through challenges and problems. It is never comfortable when you're in the middle of adversity or challenge, but when you get through it, you can look back and see what you have learnt from the situation. Any mistakes we make are simply an opportunity to grow and learn.

reflection.

Q. How can you increase your resilience?

Healthy relationships
Participation
Communication (someone to talk to)
Overcoming problems, not giving up
Standing up for what you believe
Taking healthy risks
Facing rejection or setbacks and trying again
Not taking things personally
Learning from your failures
Getting information to understand what you're facing
Adapting to new situations easily
Being honest about your fears
Figuring out who you are and what you want out of life, and not giving up on it
Persevering no matter what
Spending time with people who handle stress well.

start

BELIE VING

in what you can offer.

'I HAVE A HOPE AND A FUTURE'

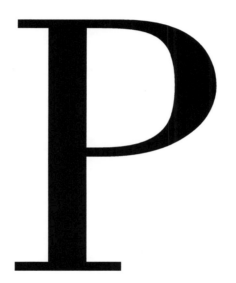

purpose.

'I HAVE A HOPE AND A FUTURE'

purpose.

SESSION SEVEN MY POTENTIAL IS LIMITLESS

outcomes.

By the end of this session, you will be able to:

RECOGNISE THE VALUE OF A POSITIVE ENVIRONMENT FOR YOUR POTENTIAL TO GROW

IDENTIFY WAYS TO BUILD YOUR CONFIDENCE

foundational concept.

POTENTIAL: possible, capable of being or becoming.

Potential is what we are capable of becoming in every area of our life. This can include friends, family, career, health, finances, personal character and attitude.

Our potential is limitless. Our potential is often in seed form. The seeds inside us are limitless. Each seed has potential to grow and become everything it was designed to be. The only thing that can limit us from becoming all that we can be is ourselves.

Living in our potential requires believing in ourselves and being confident in who we are. Our potential will not grow or be realised unless we choose to put action to it.

"Your potential is really up to you. It doesn't matter what others might think. It doesn't matter where you came from. It doesn't even matter what you might have believed about yourself at a previous time in your life. It's about what lies within you and whether you can bring it out."[1]

JOHN C. MAXWELL

1 Maxwell, J.C (2007), *Talent is Never Enough*, (pg 18) Tennessee: Thomas Nelson

reflection.

Q. What do you believe about yourself?

_____

_____

_____

_____

_____

_____

_____

_____

_____

_____

_____

Q. How do we look after our seeds of greatness?

- We nurture the seeds by valuing ourselves
- Create the right environment to bring forth the life we want – surround ourselves with healthy relationships, positive role models, and encouraging people
- Being positive and believing in our potential
- Giving ourselves opportunity to develop and try new things
- Keeping our health in balance – physically, emotionally, mentally, spiritually

We can live our life as a garden. What grows is what we plant, and what we let others plant in it. We can choose what seeds we plant in our own garden. Seeds can be skills, knowledge, experiences, thoughts and ideas.

confidence.

CONFIDENCE: full trust: belief in the trustworthiness or reliability of a person or thing, boldness, self-assurance and poise.

Confidence comes from embracing who we are. To live in our potential sometimes requires us to step out of our comfort zone and do new things. How confident we grow is our choice. A key to living in our potential is choosing to believe in ourselves and be confident. To get something we don't have, sometimes we need to do something we haven't done before.

Q. Where is our confidence found?

_____

_____

_____

_____

_____

_____

_____

_____

_____

_____

Q. Are we born with it?

_____
_____
_____
_____
_____
_____

Q. What are some things that can hinder you from growing in your potential?

_____
_____
_____
_____
_____
_____
_____

Q. Identify the seeds in your life. What can you do with these seeds starting today?

_____

_____

_____

_____

_____

_____

_____

_____

_____

_____

_____

_____

_____

_____

'I HAVE A HOPE AND A FUTURE'

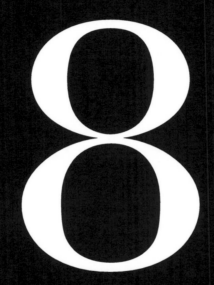

purpose.

SESSION EIGHT MY LIFE HAS PURPOSE

outcomes.

By the end of this session, you will be able to:

IDENTIFY PERSONAL DESIRES AND STRENGTHS

DEVELOP AN UNDERSTANDING THAT YOU HAVE SOMETHING TO CONTRIBUTE

foundational concept.

We are unique; there is no one else like us. How we are designed, our passions, our talents, and our strengths are unique to each of us and have purpose. All these qualities are in us so that we can fulfil our personal desires. There is a blueprint inside all of us. We are purpose-built and exist for a reason. There is a purpose for our life.

Discovering our purpose is a key aspect to every person's journey. We get a taste of our purpose when we tap into the desires of our heart. What satisfies us and what makes us frustrated? We each have a specific wiring with a palette of gifts and strengths that are as unique to each individual as a thumbprint!

Developing our gifts and talents, identifying our dreams and desires and learning how to use them, all help us to live a life of purpose. Purpose enables us to make a difference in our world. Life does not have to be about just living for ourselves. Our life can be used to make a difference for others.

We can choose to live in a world that is about ourselves or we can choose to include others in our world and make a difference.

reflection.

Q. What is your heart song?

The world we live in can try to label us, put titles on us and make us try and fit into a certain box, telling us 'This is the way to be significant, popular or successful'.

In the movie 'Happy Feet', young Mumble's song was not singing, but tap dancing. This is what he was born to do, yet his behaviour was 'un-penguin' like. We all have a song to sing. We all have a message over our life, a reason for our existence, and a purpose to our life.

By being true to ourselves, we can find our heart song and use it to create a difference in the world.
In turn, others have the choice to do the same.

_____

_____

_____

_____

_____

_____

_____

_____

_____

read the following speech from

MARTIN LUTHER KING JR.[2]

"I want to ask you a question, and that is: What is your life's blueprint? Whenever a building is constructed, you usually have an architect who draws a blueprint and that blueprint serves as a pattern,
as the guide, and a building is not well erected without a good solid blueprint.

Now, each of you is in the process of building the structure of your lives, and the question is whether you have a proper,
a solid and a sound blueprint.

I want to suggest some things which should be in your life's blueprint. Number one, in your life's blueprint, should be a deep belief in your own dignity, your worth, and your own somebodiness. Don't allow anybody to make you feel that you're nobody. Always feel that you count. Always feel that you have worth and always feel that your life has ultimate significance.

Secondly, in your life's blueprint, you must have as the basic principle the determination to achieve excellence in your various fields of endeavor. You're going to be deciding as the days, as the years unfold what you will do in life-
what your life's work will be. Set out to do it well."

Martin Luther King, Jr. speech to students at Barratt Junior High School in Philadelphia October 26, 1967.

2 Martin Luther King Jr., [Online] Available: www.drmartinlutherkingjr.com/whatisyourlifesblueprint.htm

"When you find purpose, you find passion. And when you find passion, it energises your talent so that you can achieve excellence." [3]

JOHN C. MAXWELL

3 Maxwell. J.C (2007), *Talent is Never Enough*, (pg 40) Tennessee: Thomas Nelson

ACTIVITY: TALENTS

TALENT: a special natural ability, qualities; a capacity for achievement or success; ability; a person who possesses unusual innate ability in some field or activity.

We have each been wonderfully made. Spend some time thinking about and celebrating your strengths, talents and abilities. What we are good at can be used to help others.

_____

_____

_____

_____

_____

_____

_____

_____

_____

_____

reflection.

Ways to identify talents. Ask yourself:

Q. What am I good at or what do people say I am good at?

_____

_____

_____

_____

_____

_____

Q. What comes naturally to me?

_____

_____

_____

_____

_____

_____

ACTIVITY: VISION
Write down any dreams that you haven't been able to imagine yourself fulfilling.
This can involve writing a vision statement for your life.

_____

_____

_____

_____

_____

_____

_____

reflection.

Q. Have you ever imagined yourself accomplishing your dreams?

_____

_____

_____

_____

_____

_____

EVER YONE

has strengths and talents

Q. Do you keep that vision of victory in front of you?

_____

_____

_____

_____

_____

_____

_____

Q. Do you most often see yourself winning or losing, succeeding or failing?

_____

_____

_____

_____

_____

_____

_____

_____

_____

example of a timeline to achieve a goal.

you are here.   STEPS TO TAKE / THINGS TO ACTION TO ACHIEVE DESIRED GOAL   goal. career. dream.

example of how to achieve a goal.

x represents your opposition.

BIRTHDAY SPEECHES

Imagine it is your birthday. What would you like people to say about you for your birthday speech? What would you like people to write about you on your birthday card?

IF...THEN...

If you achieved a particular goal you are working towards, then what would you do? How would your life be different as a result? How would you change? What would you do differently from then on?

WHAT MATTERS

What do you really want, deep down inside? What matters to you, in the big picture? What do you want to stand for? What do you want to do with your brief time on this planet?

CURRENT ACTIVITY

Is there anything in your life right now that gives you a sense of meaning, purpose, vitality? Anything you do that feels like you're using your time on this planet in a way that matters?

CLARIFYING VALUES

USE THIS HANDOUT FOR IDEAS ON MAKING A DREAM COLLAGE[4]

4 Source: Ideas and information in the Clarifying Values chart derived from BodyMatters Australasia, www.bodymatters.com.au

LIKES

If you had the total approval and admiration of everyone, regardless of what you do, what would you do with your life?

CHILDHOOD DREAMS

As a child, what sort of person did you imagine you would become? How did you imagine your life to be? What were your childhood dreams?

ROLE MODELS

What role models do you look up to? Who inspires you? What personal strengths or qualities do they have that you admire?

LIFE & DEATH

Imagine your own funeral. What would you like people to say about you for your eulogy or obituary? What would you like to be known for?

CHARACTER STRENGTHS

What personal strengths and qualities do you already have? Which ones would you like to develop? How would you like to apply them?

WEALTH

Imagine you win the lottery or inherit a fortune. How would you spend it? Who would you share it with?

stick your dream collage here!

Remember: If money, time, place, ability, education and confidence were not an issue, what would you do with your life?
(If you knew you could not fail, what would you do?)

watch out for

DREAM STEALERS!

FEAR

SELF-DOUBT

NEGATIVE COMMENTS

CHALLENGING CIRCUMSTANCES

LACK OF CONFIDENCE

LACK OF MOTIVATION

DISTRACTION (TOO BUSY TO FOCUS ON YOURSELF AND WHAT MAKES YOU HAPPY)

LACK OF SELF-VALUE (BELIEVING OTHER THINGS ARE MORE IMPORTANT THAN YOU)

'I HAVE A HOPE AND A FUTURE'

purpose.

SESSION NINE SHINE!

outcomes.

By the end of this session, you will be able to:

DESCRIBE WHAT YOU HAVE LEARNT

reflection.

Q. What do you stand for or what kind of declaration would you like to make over your life?

I am valuable

I am one-of-a-kind

I am wonderfully made

I have the power of choice

My decisions determine my destination

I have resilience

My potential is limitless

My life has purpose

A TEA CUP
story

"A couple went into an antique shop one day and found a beautiful teacup sitting on a shelf. They took it off the shelf, so they could look at it more closely, and said, "We really want to buy this gorgeous cup."

All of the sudden, the teacup began to talk, saying, "I wasn't always like this. There was a time when I was just a cold, hard, colourless lump of clay. One day my master picked me up and said, 'I could do something with this.' Then he started to pat me, and roll me, and change my shape.

"I said, 'What are you doing? That hurts. I don't know if I want to look like this! Stop!' But he said, 'Not yet.'

"Then he put me on a wheel and began to spin me around and around and around, until I screamed, 'Let me off, I am getting dizzy!' 'Not yet,' he said.

"Then he shaped me into a cup and put me in a hot oven. I cried, 'Let me out! It's hot in here, I am suffocating.' But he just looked at me through that little glass window and smiled and said, 'Not yet.'

"When he took me out, I thought his work on me was over, but then he started to paint me. I couldn't believe what he did next. He put me back into the oven, and I said, 'You have to believe me, I can't stand this! Please let me out!' But he said, 'Not yet.'

"Finally, he took me out of the oven and set me up on a shelf where I thought he had forgotten me. Then one day he took me off the shelf and held me before a mirror. I couldn't believe my eyes, I had become a beautiful teacup that everyone wants to buy."

Author unknown

recommended readings:

Buzan, T. (2002), *How to Mind Map*, Thorsons, HarperCollins Publishers

Chapman, G., (1995), *The Five Love Languages: The Secret to Love That Lasts*, Moody Press, U.S.

Hamilton, M. (2008), *What's Happening to Our Girls? Too much, too soon: How our kids are overstimulated, oversold and oversexed*, The Penguin Group, Australia

Holland, B. (1997), *Those Tracks on My Face*. Random House Australia

Kristof, N. and WuDunn, S. (2009), *Half the Sky: Turning Oppression into Opportunity for Women Worldwide*, Alfred, A. Knopf, New York, Random House

Warren, R. (2002), *The Purpose Driven Life*, Zondervan, Michigan

THIS IS TO CERTIFY THAT...

i have and will always have...

WORTH!

BODY AND SOUL, I AM WONDERFULLY MADE! I AM SOMEBODY!! I HAVE IMMEASURABLE VALUE.
I am unique, matchless & incomparable; no one in the ENTIRE world at present or in
ALL the ages of time has my great gifts, abilities, heart or talents.
What a woman I AM... no one has been me & no one will EVER be like me.
Because I AM WORTH TAKING CARE OF MYSELF, I remind myself & the world that "I AM A MASTERPIECE!"
There is nobody like me & there will never be anyone like me. I can't fit into anybody else's mould. I can't be compared
to anyone... not even my sister, mother or friends. My WORTH is not related to my performance & what I do – but to my
very being. My WORTH cannot be earned. It is inborn. I was born with this immeasurable value!!

i have and will always have...

STRENGTH!

My strength comes when I use my self-control for good, for myself & for others.
Choosing safe friends, good decision-making (with my mind & not from my feelings) which empowers me to
ACT & not REACT. The quality of my life is a direct result of MY choices. Stop. Think. Choose.

i have and will always have...

PURPOSE!

MY LIFE COUNTS. I AM UNIQUE! I HAVE PURPOSE.
I am custom made, a masterpiece, one-of-a-kind. I will be the best ME that I can be. I have to realise that if I'm going to
succeed; failing can be a part of the journey... the important part to remember is to not stay down!

never a failure, always a lesson.

I will learn from my mistakes & move forward. It doesn't matter where I've been; It's where I'm going that counts!
I am able to rise above any circumstance & turn it into good!